Let's Skip-Count

by Kari Jenson Gold

STECK-VAUGHN
A Harcourt Company

www.steck-vaughn.com

Instead of counting one by one,
give skip-counting a try.

0   1   2   3   4

Skip-counting can be easy and quick.
Turn the page and find out why!

6   7   8   9   10

What's an easy way to count these shoes?
To count these shoes, skip-count by twos.

0   1   2   3   4

Instead of counting one by one,
skip-count and you'll soon be done.

5   6   7   8

Let's count by twos again.
Can you skip-count to ten?

0   1   2   3   4

Instead of counting one by one,
skip-count and you'll soon be done.

6　7　8　9　10

We can watch as each dolphin dives,
To count these dolphins, skip-count by fives.

0   1   2   3   4   5

Instead of counting one by one,
skip-count and you'll soon be done.

6 7 8 9 **10**

Let's count by fives again.
Can you skip-count past ten?

Instead of counting one by one,
skip-count and you'll soon be done.

15 20 25

What's an easy way to count these hens?
To count these hens, skip-count by tens.

Instead of counting one by one,
skip-count and you'll soon be done.

30   40   50

Should you count the pennies by tens, fives, or twos?
To skip-count them, which way would you choose?

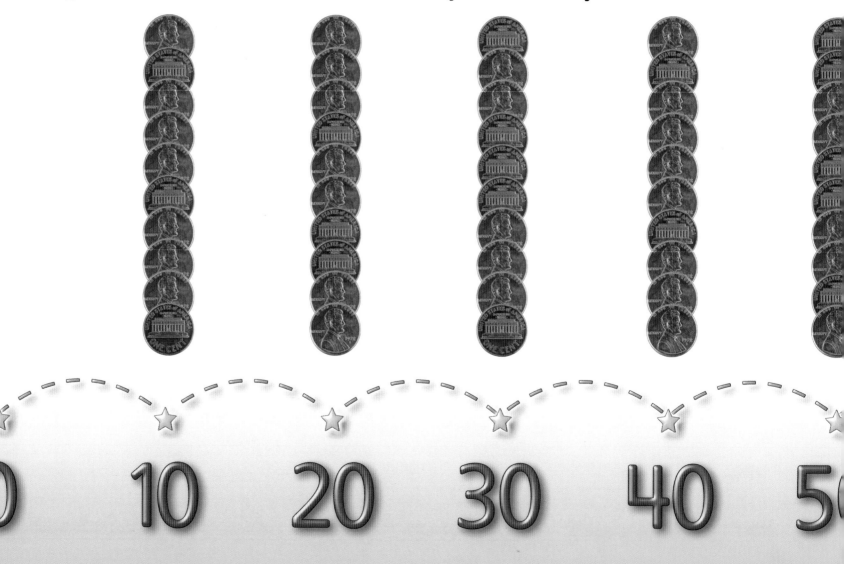

Instead of counting one by one,
skip-count and you'll soon be done.

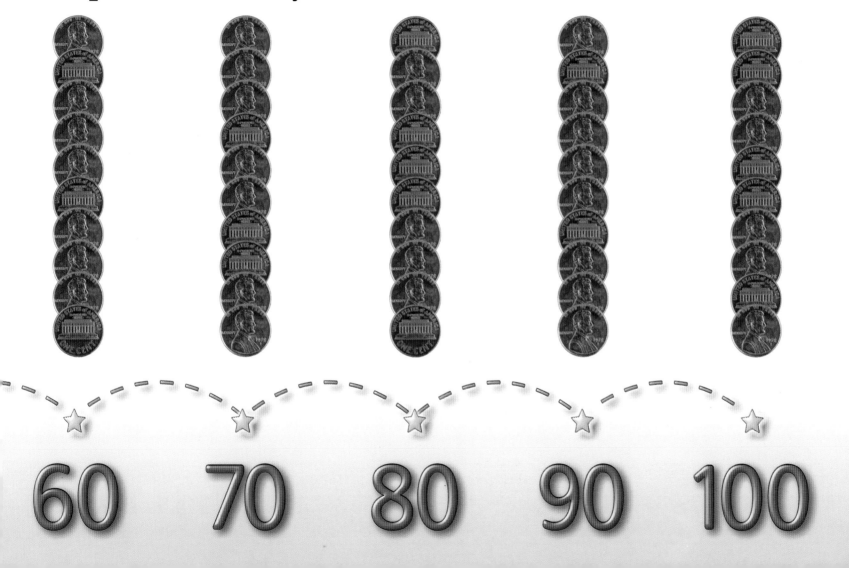

60   70   80   90   100

There's so much to count both far and near.
Can you skip-count all the chicks you see here?

0 1 2 3 4 5 6 7 8 9 10